# RELEASE TO BE RELEASED

*A story of Insecurity, Growth, and*

*Restoration*

ELLA M. JONES

Publisher: Trinity Publishing Co

Cover Design:

Printed in the United States of America

ISBN # 978-1-64153-349-2

# ACKNOWLEDGEMENTS

## Minister Marcus Jones. Sr. -

Thank you for being an awesome Husband, Intercessor, Protector, and my Covering. You lift me up when I'm down, and never hesitate to have a praise party. You have been my biggest cheerleader, my go-to guy with no pity party allowed. The greatest part is doing ministry with you in Yielded Vessels Ministries. Thank you for allowing me to be me while supporting the adventures God sends my way.

## Gustava Barnett -

Thank you for being a mother that wants nothing but the best for her daughter. You have been my 'Book-Pusher,' telling each of your friends and associates about my previous book as well as this one prior to the release. You are very supportive, and encouraging while showing genuine love.

## Sisters and Brothers in Christ -

Thank you for the push, encouragement, and support.

Last, but definitely not least, I give all the glory to my Lord and Savior, Jesus Christ.

# CONTENTS

# NOT GOOD ENOUGH

Have you ever felt like you were not good enough?

Was it due to things you had been told, or did you compare yourself to others and felt you didn't measure up?

When we feel 'not good enough', we have a tendency to allow things to happen in our lives that we normally would not. We are more accepting of the negative than the positive because we do not feel we deserve anything good.

Things that have happened in our past can be the reason for our insecurity and low self-esteem. We have a choice of dealing with things of the past that can help build us up by letting go of what was, or we can keep holding on to it and continue to allow it to control our future.

When we tell ourselves we are not good enough, and we act in a manner that will let others know we do not feel good enough, it is an insult to God. He created us in His image. We are telling Him, He didn't do a good enough job.

# GROWING UP

## TOO BLACK. TOO UGLY. TOO SKINNY.

---

Going through the motions while hurting inside.

I do not know if I hid the anger on the inside or if it just went unnoticed.

I wonder if anyone ever wondered why is she so mean and hatful. Why does she prefer to be by herself, and push people away? I would only allow people to get to a certain place with me, and I would start to distance myself. In some ways, I still do that when I feel it is necessary.

As a young girl I had a neighbor friend named Evelyn. We would ride our bikes and play together in our cute little rompers that tie on the shoulder. How funny is it that, I remember the small details of my childhood?

When I got tired of being around Evelyn I would become mean to her so she would leave me alone. She was just as mean, so we would both run in the house angry, until the next day.

I think we got along because we were a lot alike and understood when enough was enough. I never experienced a friendship where we had to be around each other all of the time and do everything together. Definitely not talk on the phone all of the time. I would have been better off back then if we had text messaging.

I was born in Shreveport, Louisiana. While my mother was pregnant with me there was a terrible house fire that killed my sister, Darlene, and my brother, Dale. Their life was lost and I was born.

Jeremiah 1:1, "Before I formed you in the womb, I knew you, before you were born, I set you apart; I appointed you as a prophet to the nations. Sovereign Lord, I said, I do not know how to speak; I am only a child."

This scripture says it all about my beginning. God knew me before I was born, and set me apart while I was in the womb. God spared my life for a reason. That is why I am uniquely me.

I had a serious fear of fire, and I never questioned why. Later in years I associated my fear of fire with the fire that happened while I was in the womb.

My family does not talk about the tragedy, so I do not have much information on Dale and Darlene. I have learned to celebrate them on my birthday, since that is when they went to heaven to be with the Lord.

However, I often wonder what it would have been like to have a big sister, and if my brother would have been protective of me.

My surviving brother is the oldest of the four children. We have a distant relationship, and we seem to be okay with that. Some may say that we need to try to get closer, and that may work for you. You might not understand, but this works for us.

Growing up, no matter how much we argued or how many fights we had, he would not allow anyone else to mess with me. A lot of people in the neighborhood knew of him and his reputation, so they did not bother me.

When I started high school, I was told to ride the bus home, and not to walk through the field. Sometimes after cheerleader practice I would save my bus fare and walk.

One of those times, as I got close to home, there was a guy that grabbed me. It was definitely God that gave me strength to fight for my life. He was pulling, trying to remove my shorts. Someone was coming! He let me go and ran.

I recognized the attacker. I remembered seeing him sitting on the porch of one of the houses I walked by. The house was noticeable because of the bus that sat out-front.

After the attack, I ran home and collapsed on the front porch. My brother came out and I told him what happened. He told mother to call the police as he took off running.

I knew he was headed for that house. He knew where the bus was that I mentioned. When the police arrived they took mother and I to the house and my brother was there fighting with the guy that attacked me. One of the police officers asked if that was the guy. Yes, that was the guy.

I do not know how my brother knew who to go after. I am not sure if I described the attacker or his clothing, but he knew someone had messed with his little sister.

The guy was arrested. I hated that I had to go to court. They made me feel like I had done something wrong because I had on shorts. I was coming home from cheerleader's practice.

I was asked if I flirted with him when I saw him on the porch. No, I hadn't and he hadn't said anything to me.

I resented being asked the questions, but I also knew I had to cooperate so that he would go to jail. I felt like the victim was being prosecuted. Going through that ordeal I can understand why some people prefer not to report these types of crimes.

It was finally over and he received three years for attempted rape. His intention to sexually assault me was stopped by someone coming by. Praise God!

I never said anything to that person, nor do I know what he did or did not do. I just ran! I never went that way again. I was obedient and caught the bus.

I grew up in Dallas, Texas, in the Oak Cliff area.

I lived with my mom, and older brother. On the weekends, I would visit my grandparents. My grandfather was a kind and funny man. He took good care of my Big Mama. No matter how angry he made her, she made sure meals were prepared.

I would often see her rub his feet, pick the bumps on his face, and many other things. I did not realize then the affect it had on me later in years. This became a learned behavior for me.

Big Daddy and I had our time together. On most weekends we ventured to Kinney shoe store. One Saturday after I had purchased my shoes from Kinney's and we were headed home. My grandfather turned the corner and my door came open. I fell out of the car. He stopped, and I remember him panicking.

I was okay, just scared with a few bruises, but I was still holding on to that shoe box. We must have laughed about that for a while!

When he passed away my Big Mama moved in with us. She ran an in-home daycare. It was great to see her give so much love and attention to the children. Some of the children even stayed overnight so their parents could work overtime, or have time to themselves.

I remember there would be ten plus children at our home at any given time. She cooked breakfast and lunch for the children and for those that stayed later, dinner was served.

My grandmother was a sweetheart. She taught me to always be a lady. Her genuine kindness was a true example of how to treat people and be good to yourself as well. She marched by her own beat and taught me to do the same.

I think about how protective she was of me. When my brother would say mean things to me, she would tell me that I am beautiful and that I can do anything I wanted to do. Although I did not always feel that way, I hung on to those words. I think it was enough to keep me off the deep end. When I was a little girl she would only let me wear white under garments to church. I never asked why but I now think it was a purity reason. Growing up, she and mother taught me to always stay clean. They would say stay covered up. Hmmm, if they saw those club clothes I would wear, they would have had a fit, per say.

It was important to them that my hair stayed cute. I knew when to speak and stay out of grown folks' business, they did not talk about people in front of us, but I ear hustled. I have seen how it can change the way the child treats that person that was talked about.

When I decided I never wanted to have children, some called it selfish and thought I would change my mind later in life. It was a decision I made no matter how other people felt about it. I am aware that if God said so, it would have been so, no matter how I felt. I just knew what I did and did not want.

As I was in Elementary and Junior High School I did okay with my grades. I would stay sick a lot with asthma, severe nose bleeds, kidney problems, and more so I did not make a lot of friends. I stayed occupied with reading, writing, and keeping my room organized. I liked to decorate.

Those in the neighborhood were family. Even with them I would only let them in to a certain point except my big sister/friend, Kay-Kay whom I currently stay in touch with regularly.

My Mother made sure I was well taken care of, and that I had all I needed and a lot of what I wanted. I was taught that household chores were not something I got paid for but it was what I was to do. The shopping and extra money I received was out of love, and to show that my help with the chores was appreciated.

Some would say I was a spoiled child, but trust me, when I did not do what I was supposed to do, I got nothing, and a punishment went with it.

Mother also showed me how to be responsible, and how to take care of bills. We would catch the #55 Lancaster bus into downtown Dallas and go from place to place paying bills. She made sure I was paying attention.

When I was about 15 or 16, mother started allowing me to go alone and handle the bills while she worked. Those of you from Dallas, or you that have been here a while, knew that there were the three B's, Burt's, Butlers, and Bakers shoe stores downtown. I was in shoe heaven. When extra was available, mother would add extra so that I could shop.

I appreciate her for teaching me responsibility in a variety of areas. The sad part is that I did not show much appreciation. I acted more like I was entitled to the nicer things and kind gestures.

The only man my mother brought around me was Mr. Leon Bagley. If there was someone else, I never knew about them. I have so many fun memories of Mr. Leon. On Saturdays, he would take us to watch the planes take off at Love Field Airport. I would get my soda and bugles, and I would enjoy the moment.

Every Christmas he would get me a new bike. There would be nothing wrong with the bike from the year before. I would also receive an Etch-A-Sketch and clothes from Mr. Leon.

I will admit that he spoiled me. That might be when I started associating gifts to love.

He was a great guy, Mr. Leon. Although he was a father figure in my life, and as much as I wanted to call him dad since I did not have a dad, my mother would not allow me to do so. He seemed like a father. He was Mr. Leon.

When mother and Mr. Leon stopped seeing each other, I missed him. I did not hear from him for years until one day he reached out to mother and got my number and he called me.

We talked a few times, and even planned for him to come over and meet my husband.

I received a call that Mr. Leon had passed away.

I was so hurt. In my mind I was about to have my father figure back. Just like that, Mr. Leon was gone but will never be forgotten.

This is the reason we must appreciate and show love to those in our lives. I will always remember him calling me 'Chicken' because of my skinny legs.

I know now that it was a term of endearment from him, but during that time it was another insecurity that I did not want to express. I went along with it because I knew he loved me. That pattern followed me through the years. I would accept things from those that I felt loved me, even if I was uncomfortable with their words and /or actions towards me.

I mentioned earlier that I was a mean person. Along with being mean, I was insecure, but as insecure as I was, I did not allow that to make me be a follower to fit in. I was still an individual that did it my way or I just did not do it at all. It did not matter to me if everyone else was doing it differently.

I have an older brother that would often remind me that I was not good enough. He would do that by telling me I was too black, too ugly, and too skinny. Those words let me know that I was not good enough. It meant more because if my big brother felt that way, surely everyone else would. When I would cry about it, mother would say, "Don't pay that boy no mind." She was not aware of the effect his words had on me. I do not think I did either.

No matter how bad our relationship was, I still remember him teaching me how to play jacks on the front porch. He was the one that taught me how to drive, because mother never drove.

Once I started middle school, I tried out for cheerleading because of what my brother said about me. I wanted to show him that I could do it. I tried out and made it in Junior High School. I was actually being a cheerleader, although I agreed with him.

In High school I tried out and made it. I cheered at one game and quit the squad. I did not fit in and was uncomfortable. I thought I was okay because I once again showed him I was good enough.

The next year I tried out for Drill team and made it. Again, I did not follow through with it. That pattern followed me for years.

I had to build up my confidence in spite of, and it has not been easy.

When I started dating it was awkward.

I thought guys only wanted to be with me for sex, and I was determined not to let that be the reason, I would get mad and talk really crazy to them, but yet again I thought I was not good enough so I was alone a lot.  The one's that was probably serious, I didn't believe them and sent them on their way. The one's I knew were no good for me were the ones I kept going back to thinking I would change them. I was really messed up.

Even with jobs, careers, education and more, I did not follow through to the end. I would get in my own way. I would do so well on a job, and I would be comfortable where I was. It did not matter to me if I was promoted to supervisor or manager, I did not feel that I was good enough.

There were times management would tell me I was leadership material, but I never put much effort in moving forward in that direction, my mind was made up that I didn't deserve it.

I always wanted to be a flight attendant. It even says it in my class year book. Delta Airlines had a write-up in the newspaper, "Hiring for Flight Attendants." I prepared for that hiring event for weeks. I got there and saw so many people, but I was determined to apply.

I did not really think I would get job. I went through the process. During that time they checked your weight and height. I was good there. They talked to us about the process of being hired, and the training that would take place in Atlanta, Georgia.

After a couple of weeks, I received the call.

I was hired! I had to prepare to go to Atlanta for three weeks. I was in there. Again, I did not follow through. I used my mother being sick at the time as an excuse to cancel my career of being a flight attendant. Understand, mother was not sick enough for me to cancel. That was my way out.

The mask of insecurity was covering well, to the point of being a lifestyle. I was hiding the hurt of being invisible while being looked at as strong; I carried the thought of not being good enough while pretending to be better than I thought, the joy of no one knowing about the pain or hurt. I was told so many times that I never would, and I never thought I could, so it was hard to celebrate when I did. It was as if I was afraid of success.

I had so many things I talked myself out of because I did not think I was good enough to complete, and afraid of what would be said if I failed, so I would go to a point and let it go before it let me go.

I like the quote that says, "You have to practice success. Success doesn't just show up. If you aren't practicing success today, you won't wake up in 20 years and be successful, because you won't have developed the habits of success, which are small things like finishing what you start, putting a lot of effort into everything you do, being on time, treating people well."

Michelle Obama

I remember the times of being told I was pretty to be so black. It would make me so angry. That was not a compliment to me. My thought was when you speak of a lighter skin woman, you do not say, "You are pretty to be light skinned." To make it even worse, a guy said to me, "I normally don't date dark skinned women, but I'll date you." Was I supposed to have been impressed by that statement? My response was, "I wouldn't date anyone that would say that." He did not understand the reason it bothered me, and I was not going to explain it. That was like explaining the pain I tried to hide.

Later in life I gained understanding of the statement, but it felt good when someone finally gave a compliment without mentioning skin tone. Oh, but now, I realize that I am a beautiful black woman and I would not have it any other way. I realize everyone has their own preference.

I once dated a lighter skinned guy, and when he got upset with me, he would call me a black this and that, which to me proved that he thought he was better than me because he was a lighter complexion. That was my mindset behind the original statement of not normally dating dark skinned women. I had to bring myself back to reality and remember my worth during times of mistreatment. Unfortunately, I would allow it to go on too long, and by the time I got fed up with the mistreatment I would be out of control, and that's when I would cut up.

When I go in to things with the mindset of what I was taught, people can accept my dos and don'ts or just walk away, which I learned was a good thing to keep me from unnecessary torment. I had an 'I don't care' mentality that helped me deal with the hurt.

I was a young girl full of anger. I did not want to be that way, but I did not know any other way. I did not have anyone that I felt comfortable with releasing what was on my heart and mind.

That is why I love being a mentor to young girls. I am able to share my experiences, and to let them know that I understand because I have been there and survived, and so will they.

My mother and grandmother never showed shame of being dark skinned. They always stood tall and demanded respect. It was as if they were saying, "I'm dark but I'm just as good as you are." I was taught to never think I am better than others, but just as good as others.

I spoke about being a sickly little girl, but my mother was not missing church unless it was urgent. That is why I know it was hard for her when 'Big Mama' became ill and she had to stay home with her.

She did it gracefully until God called my grandmother home. She planted a seed. I miss her so much. She was a joy to be around. She might be gone, but she will never be forgotten.

Sundays, we attended church from sun up to sun down, and it did not bother me because that is all I knew. I started out in the youth choir, and I was the youth Sunday School Secretary, which was scary for me because I did not like being out front.

I would have to read the minutes during Sunday school, and I was so nervous. The director, Ms. Barbara Hall, would make me feel at ease. She was one of the nicest ladies I have ever known.

After choir rehearsals I would wait until everyone had cleared out before leaving so no one would notice me. I did not want to be the scene of attention.

I enjoyed being at church, but I hate that I did not let anyone in. I might have gotten the help needed with the insecurity and lack of confidence that was inside of me.

I would ride the church van, and I hated when he got to my house because I did not want anyone looking at me as I exited the van. Truth be told, I do not think anyone paid attention. I was so mean I did not want them saying bye to me, when they did, I would mumble back and run into the house.

As a choir, we would sing at many 3:00 services, musicals, revivals, etc. We had a great time at Youth for Christ nights. We loved rocking our choir robes and representing Bexar Street Baptist Church. I loved all that. I did not have to socialize one on one.

I ask myself if I am happy that no one knew about the pain I carried inside because it kept me from being talked about or looked at as crazy. Oddly enough I am happy that I did not speak up. I do not believe it was my time to come out of it. I say that because of the lessons I got from it. Others might say I would have been better off having someone to talk to. I might have turned out to be a better person, but I do not know if I would be the person I am today. I like her.

Some things were just never discussed, such as my father being the reason for the fire that killed my brother and sister, Dale and Darlene. My mother has never talked to me about it, and she will not, so I just leave it alone to avoid upsetting her. I received a few details from my brother, and that is where it ends. I can only imagine what's locked up inside of them after never speaking of such tragedy.

I often wonder if all the trouble my brother went through was a result of witnessing the loss of his little sister and brother.

I never met my father until I graduated from High School. He showed up. I do not even know how he knew I was graduating and where we lived. I wondered if mother somehow contacted him to let him know his only child was graduating. My older brother and I had different dads. I never asked and she never said if she had or not. As you can tell there was a lack of communication.

My attitude was so bad towards him; he left immediately after the ceremony without even a good bye.

I did not hear from him again until one day over 20 years later. My mother called to tell me that my father's doctor had Red Cross looking for me because he was dying and asked to see me. I could not believe it. I did not understand why he wanted me to come see him.

I was refusing to go and could not understand why my mother, the woman who was physically abused by him throughout the marriage until the day of the fire.

I finally agreed to go to Arkansas and see him at the hospital. I arrived at the hospital and walked in to his room. He just looked at me. I finally asked if he knew who I was and he said, "Ella Marie" then he stated, "Your mother is crazy."

That made me angry. Why in the world would that be the next thing out of his mouth to his daughter who he had not seen but once in her whole life?

I told him he was the one crazy. He smiled and that was the end of our conversation. We never said another word to one another the four days I was there at the hospital with him.

His friends and family came in and out of that hospital room. I told them who I was and no one said anything else to me, they would tell him they were going to eat and would be back. No one offered to bring me anything back to eat or ask me to join them to get out of the hospital for a while.

His nurse asked me where was I from. I told her that I rode the Greyhound bus from Dallas, and that I did not know anyone there in town.

She told me she had me covered for breakfast, lunch and dinner in the cafeteria for the duration of my stay. Her kindness and consideration had me in tears.

I did not understand why I was being treated with such negativity from my dad's family, but I figured it was due to whatever story he told them.

I finally left and went home. I did not get the apology I thought I would receive. I'm not sure what I wanted him to say, but I definitely did not think I would get silence. I can't even explain why I did not say anything else or ask questions. I wonder if he would have given me some answers that I can't get from anyone else.

He passed away a couple of days later. I was contacted and informed of the funeral home to receive more information.

I called and found out when the funeral was. Mother and I drove down for the service.

We arrived and were preparing to sit down when the funeral director asked me to get in line and march in with the family. I wanted to laugh at him, but I stayed in order and got in line. The young lady that I was told he raised as a daughter, stood in front of me. The director stated that I was the oldest and I would go in first.

The young lady started to act a fool so I told him it did not matter to me. He said, "Decent, and in order." I went in first. It was the most uncomfortable position I had ever been in.

After the service was over, a few people recognized my mother from the time she lived in Arkansas, before moving to Louisiana with my father.

As we were speaking to them while heading out the door to go to the cemetery, we discovered that the funeral directors and some of the family members were gone already with the body. They never said we are leaving or anything. We changed clothes and hit the road back to Dallas.

About a month later, the young lady he raised contacted me about moving to Dallas. She needed a place to stay until she got on her feet. I was in total disbelief that she would call me for such a large favor, especially after the way she acted at the funeral. "I don't even know you," I told her. I politely asked her not to contact me again.

Not long afterwards, I remember receiving a letter asking me to contact the Social Security office, which I did. They asked me to send a copy of my birth certificate. There was an open fraud case.

Apparently, the young lady that my dad raised had applied and received my father's social security benefits, but I was his only surviving biological child. I sent what was requested and everything was settled on my end. However, charges were brought against her. I do not know what happened after that. I was curious as to why they did not ask her for proof as they asked me; the person that did not even file for his benefits.

————————•••●●••————————

# EDUCATION

Proverbs 23:12 Apply your heart to instructions and ear to words of knowledge.

My education is definitely a variety. I was due to graduate from High School in 1980, but due to missing too many days, and being behind,

I was missing some credits so I did not graduate with my class. However, I did not give up.

I went back to school the following school year, part time and completed what I needed.

I graduated in 1981 from Roosevelt High School.

My time at Roosevelt is almost like a blur. I did not make many friends, and I did not participate much in extracurricular activities besides the Pep Rallies and a few football games.

I would attend but I really do not remember being with anyone. I was just there.

After high school I attended Allstate Business School where I learned typing, shorthand, and business management.

From Allstate I attended El Centro College taking my basic courses, and on to the University of North Texas. There I took classes, not knowing what I wanted to major in at the time. Due to an incident of self-defense I was released for a semester and never returned.

I later attended Everest College and received my Associates Degree in Criminal Justice. This is also where I met my husband, Marcus.

I am grateful for Biblical Studies at Southern Bible Institute and College. I look forward to going back for the knowledge.

I had a strong interest in being a Funeral Director. I attended Dallas Institute of Funeral Services for a short while, until I became ill.

I received my certification in Life Coaching in 2019 from New Skills Academy.

I am presently taking classes to get my mentoring certification. The more I know the more I grow.

———————•••●●•••———————

# MARRIAGE

Ephesians 4:2-3, be completely humble and gentle; be patient, bearing one with another in love. Make every effort to keep the unity of the Spirit through the bond of peace.

In 1984 I got married and thought I was living life. He bought me anything I wanted. I always had a nice car and a nice place to live. I dressed nice, etc. The Jheri curl I wore was always on point! Yes, I had a curl.

Everyone saw a great couple, a spoiled wife, and a hard-working man. No one saw the controlling spirit. I did not care that he said do not leave the house, as long as I could shop. I did not care that he did not want me to talk to my friends that he referred to as the jealous friends that hated that I was with him, as long as he paid all the bills.

I shut out the few friends I had to make him happy. The most hurtful thing was when I would visit my mother. There were no cell phones back then, and he would call her home phone after I had only been there for a short time and tell me it was time for me to come home, and I would leave. I could see the hurt in my mother's eyes.

When he said do not go anywhere, he made sure of it by loosening the battery on the car. He just did not understand that once he said it, I was not leaving. When he said do not talk to anyone, I was not going to talk to anyone. That did not stop him from taking the phones with him when he left. I put up with these things because he took care of me financially. There was no physical abuse, so I thought I was not to be compared to the women that were being beaten. I did not know about mental abuse at the time.

No one knew what was happening in my home because I did not talk about it. I was taught by my Big Mama that you do not speak against your spouse. Do not share your marriage information so I did not share anything.

Everyone thought I was the happiest woman around; all the while I was hurting inside. I refused to share the pain with anyone. I made sure I kept up the façade. Now, do not get me wrong, I was not perfect. I had a bad attitude, fowl mouth, selfish, and more. I was not a good cook. As a matter of fact, he preferred to do the cooking, which I did not mind. He criticized everything I did. It seems that I could not do anything right, which was confirmation of things that I was told as a kid. He knew how to make me feel like a queen when amongst others.

He took care of me when I was ill so I thought that meant he loved me, but he just cared. I learned there was a difference. While together, I dealt with Meningitis which kept me in the hospital for an extended period of time. Another traumatic experience was when my appendix ruptured, spreading poison all over my body. That day in 1984 we discovered I had a tubal pregnancy. This had me out of commission for a while. Had he or she been born, I would have a 36-year-old man or woman calling me mother.

I was advised that I could still have kids, but as I stated earlier, I did not want any children. I do not know why I had to go through that. Whether I wanted a baby or not, I was hurt. I wondered if I was being punished for saying I did not want any children. We never discussed this and he never said anything to me about the illness or aftercare. I know it was frustrating for him, but we did not talk about it.

I often wondered if he talked with or complained to others about this situation.

How many of you know that when someone is trying to control your every move, there is something they want to keep you from knowing? This was the case for me.

One day my ex-husband brought home a beautiful baby girl and told me that her mother did not want the responsibility, and he wanted to be a good father, so he took on the responsibility.

In case you are wondering, no there was no discussion with me. He decided that I would change my work schedule so I could take her to day care and pick her up. We shopped for all her needs and went on as if there was nothing wrong with the picture.

Questions like, "Whose baby is this?" We answered, "It is our baby". Nothing more was said. Things went on as a happy family for a while. That was until I started feeling like a single mother. He was not coming home until he was ready. When I would ask what was going on, he felt that as long as bills were paid, needs were met, I should be fine. It definitely was not the fault of the baby girl, and I never treated her as such.

Enough was enough. I finally walked away. I just could not take it anymore. I knew if I stayed much longer I was going to become more attached to this little girl, and it would be much harder to leave. I could not stay for the sake of this child while being mentally and verbally abused, which I did not know to even call it that until years later. I knew she would be safe, and he was going to make sure she would be taken care of.

Remember, I never spoke against him, so when I left I was looked at as the bad person, or I must be crazy to leave a good man that did everything for me. I never tried to explain or defend myself. I left it all, even clothes. I just wanted my peace of mind.

I wasn't sure if I would ever get married again, but God sent me a mind changer. I met Marcus in 2006, after I transferred to Everest College where he was attending. He laughs when I tell him that the day he walked into the class room I heard, "That's him!" I said, "Lord if that's you let it be," and so it is! I can say this with joy in my heart and a peace of mind.

Our romance went kind of quickly once we established a relationship. We had a non-traditional wedding. I did not say yes to the dress. I said yes to the denim suit.

We asked all of our friends and family to wear denim. There was no wedding time. The ceremony was held during Sunday morning service, so you just had to come to church. Praise and worship went forth, baptism of the children, and communion was extended. Pastor G's sermon and our vows were our union into our new beginning together.

The proposal was also non-traditional. I was giving Marcus a pedicure. He looked at me and said let's set a date. After making sure that he was talking about getting married, I picked up a calendar. He said the last Sunday in that year, which was December 30th 2007. We started making a few simple plans, and God made it happen.

It has not always been easy. There have been some hard times, but we hung in there. Not because we had to, but because we wanted to.

Our marriage was God ordained and we had to believe that God would see us through it all. We are not perfect, but we serve a perfect God together.

Our story is interesting. We grew up in the same neighborhood, but did not know one another. There was a point where we attended the same church, and did not know one another. God kept us apart until it was time.

I am the bonus mom to Marcus' five children. Two are his biological children, and the three others you can't tell him they are not his children. He shows no difference between either of them. Then there's me, with no children, and used to having everything to myself.

This made a difficult situation for a while. The children were used to being there with him; lying around watching movies, all getting his attention. I wanted him to myself. There were some attitudes and misunderstandings going on.

What made things worse, we did not properly communicate. We did not sit down and talk about it until things got heated, and by then it was anger, and a total disconnect.

I missed out on being an example to the girls. Mentoring them and being their go- to-person. This is one reason why mentoring is so important to me now. We also missed out on showing them all how to handle marriage with communication, openness and togetherness.

Marcus was in a position of trying to please me, which caused a separation with his children.

There was also the case of Marcus trying to please the children, which caused a disconnection in our relationship. It was a difficult time, but a real-life lesson.

Once we started praying more, and allowing God in all things, life became better. Although we are not where we would like to be with the children, we continue to pray for them, and he has talked to them about the mistakes made. It is one of those things where you have to admit your part, forgive yourself, and go where it leads.

In marriage you have to keep other people out of your ups and downs. Marriage is between you, your spouse and God. You can't run to family and friends when things are not going well.

When you talk negatively about your spouse to them, and when the two of you work it out, you are good and those you talked to about your spouse still has the residue of what you said on them. I do not have a problem with marriage counseling.

However, I do believe the person should be equipped for the task and someone that can and will hear both sides without making judgments. I would prefer someone that does not know the couple on a personal level.

Communication is a large part of a successful marriage. You can't hold things in to avoid an argument. You can't just go along to get along. You must express yourself to avoid the resentment. Now, understand there has to be some compromise, but do not lose yourself trying to please your spouse or others.

Marcus and I have been blessed to work together in ministry, and it draws us closer together. God has work for us to do, and I am blessed to be doing it with my best friend. Marriage is what you make of it. You definitely have to keep God first.

We stay true to our vows of loving and respecting one another. I make sure I carry myself in a manner that honors our marriage. I show respect when he is around and when he is not. He does the same for me. We love to do little things that do not cost a lot of money but mean the most to us.

We are not extravagant people, so we have a few favorite places we like to go and enjoy one another as long as we are together.

We visit a place called Prayer Mountain a lot. Prayer Mountain is a place of peace. Each time we go, we have a special time with the Lord. I also enjoy the praise and worship that breaks out in our home at any given moment.

I definitely had to separate the two marriages. I could not bring my dirt from marriage one into marriage two. When Marcus saw that happening, he would quickly say, "I did not do it, stop trying to make me pay for it." I had to get some 'act right' in my spirit to avoid losing a good man.

Anything worth having is worth working for. We put in the work required.

# UN-EQUALLY YOKED

2nd Corinthians 6:14 do not be unequally yoked with unbelievers. For what partnership has righteousness with lawlessness? Or what fellowship has light with darkness?

When we hear the words equally yoked, we immediately think marriage, but I believe it applies in any relationship, or friendship, it is going to be difficult if you are not on the same page, going in the same direction, able to work together on the same agenda. When we are in any kind of relationship with those that we are not equally in yoke with, instead of working together, we will be in conflict.

I was always told to be with those that are on the same path as yourself, but I did not know what path I was on, so it did not matter to me which way they were going. I felt I had no right to remove anyone, when I was the one that needed to be removed.

I realized that at times I was spending time with those that did not want me to move forward, those that allowed me to act a fool without saying, "You are wrong, or you are out of order."

These people enjoyed the foolishness that came forth, and the actions that was not of God. I can't blame them, because I allowed it. When we know better we do better. I had to start doing better for myself.

Speaking of unequally yoked, the first time I got married, it was with someone I was not equally yoked with. He had never attended church, and I was in church every chance I could get.

He started going to church with me, but the church was not in him. He knew how to play the role when in the presence of the right people.

We did not have much in common. I do not remember us having any meaningful conversations. He said what we were doing, how it was to be done, and that was that.

You may ask, why did you marry him, and why did you stay. Truth is, he provided the material things I wanted and thought I needed at the time, and I didn't think I could have those things on my own. Wow, I was so shallow.

I have had those I call acquaintances that were cool with me if I went out with them or talked bad about someone with them, but as soon as I said no, or stopped participating in the conversation and letting them know that it is wrong, things changed.

I guess that is why those people never made it past acquaintances. Unequally Yoked.

I have learned to surround myself with those I can learn from and grow with. Those that are on the path of righteousness, and we can hold one another accountable, the one's that will call me on my foolishness, and not take it to others behind my back.

I am so grateful for those with the same set of values, that love the Lord, and do not mind praising and worshipping Him.

I am so grateful for friends that respect where I am, even if their faith is higher. They walk with me to increase my faith. This is what I call Equally Yoked.

# PARTY TIME

**Ephesians** 5:18, and do not get drunk with wine, for that is debauchery, but be filled with the spirit....

I think about how many times this scripture has been used as an excuse to have a drink and feel good about it, and how many times the line has been crossed.

I was a party girl. I started going to clubs at the age of 18. After the first night of fun I had to be in the midst. For me it was not about the drinking and definitely not about drugs, but it was about feeling free. I would drink minimally, and until this day I have never done drugs that were not prescribed.

I saw what drugs could do to you through family members and that put a 'No Way' in me that I could never explain, and a 'No' that I am glad about.

I would just dance the night away, I am not sure if I was a good dancer or not, I just know that I enjoyed being on the dance floor. I didn't have to talk nor deal with anything, just dancing.

I got to the point of going to the club Wednesday thru Sunday. Yes, I was still going to church, singing in the choir, going to revivals, and more. I used the excuse that I was still giving God some time. SMH

The club was my way of getting away from things I needed to deal with. I later learned that no matter what the issue would still be there once I stopped dancing.

I danced with a broken heart.

I danced afraid of my tomorrow.

I danced needing a financial breakthrough.

I danced when I lost the job.

I danced when I felt betrayed.

I danced when I felt I had it all together.

Now I dance for Jesus, and all that is listed above is given to Him to handle.

I remember birthday #42. I did not have any plans, and no one called to hang out. I was determined not to stay home alone. I got dressed and took myself out. I never had a problem going out alone.

I dated myself often; dinner, movies, and a walk in the park. However, on this night I had a terrible time. I was not in the mood to dance.

My attitude was bad. I did not want to be bothered with anyone, but I refused to go home.

I sat in a corner trying to understand what was happening. I finally convinced myself that it was best to go home. Once in the car I said, "I hear you Lord." I was not supposed to be there. That place was not the answer.

I asked Him to bless me to make it home safely and show me another way.

Once I made it home I cried out for better; a better me, a better way of handling issues, and most of all a better relationship with Him.

I went out a few times here and there afterwards for a friend's birthday or some kind of celebration, but I would not have a good time partying, although I enjoyed being there with them celebrating the occasion.

I no longer had the desire of the environment. I had to get to the point of wanting the change. Even now, when invited to a celebration, I need to know where it is held, what will be happening, etc. I have a changed mind.

# MENTOR

1st Thessalonians 2:8, So, being affectionately desirous of you, we were ready to share with you not only the gospel of God but also our own selves, because you had become very dear to us.

I have been blessed to be the Founder and Director of the Ruth and Naomi Youth Mentoring Program. I also have the pleasure of being one of the mentors. We are committed to helping young ladies develop from a caterpillar to butterfly. We are there for them during the process of growth and change, their metamorphosis.

The process of growth is timely. The caterpillar goes through four stages to grow into a butterfly from the egg, larva, pupa and adult.

The caterpillar starts with hanging upside down from a leaf and spins itself a cocoon, a protective casing. That is when the transformation begins.

In order for the caterpillar to become a butterfly, it has to go through the process. It does not skip a step. It has to go through to completion.

That is where the mentor steps in to assist them with the process, as they learn to protect themselves by not sharing. The mentors must allow them to get comfortable enough to share any hurt, pain, or ask any needed questions. We have to be able to share how we dealt with a variety of issues that may arise during the process.

Being a mentor is rewarding and satisfying.

I love when the mentees share how they have been helped, and demonstrate how they are using the tools provided to be a better person.

We have those that were having a hard time with a certain issue and opened up enough to be guided in the right direction. It feels good when you build a bond that makes the mentees comfortable enough to share their troubles, and the look they have when you share your experience in that area.

Our purpose as mentors is to empower and inspire, along with motivating them by setting goals with a mindset to succeed.

We as mentors encourage the mentees to have a Can-Do Spirit. In mentoring I believe that we have to be consistent in our rapport with the young ladies.

We let each of them know that we are there for them; although it may be voluntary it is a commitment.

Every Ruth could use a Naomi and every Naomi could help a Ruth. The story in the bible about Ruth, Naomi and Orpah tells of the story of heartache and disappointment. Naomi lost her husband and sons. Ruth and Orpah lost their husbands.

Ruth decided to follow Naomi into her country, although Naomi originally objected. In Ruth 1:6, Ruth replied, "Don't urge me to leave you or to turn back from you. Where you go, I will go and where you stay, I will stay. Your people will be my people and your God my God."

We are someone's Naomi and someone's Ruth.

There are those that we must mentor and guide and there are those that must mentor and guide us.

There is a blessing in pushing someone to be the best of their self and have those that push us to be the best of ourselves.

In mentoring we must care about the well-being of others and sow our time into their lives. Teach and be teachable. Be who God called you to be to them.

Mentoring has made me a better person. For a very long time I did not share my story with others, but now I love to share my story with the young ladies to let them know that I too have been there.

I allow them to ask questions. I am open and honest with them and although I believe that things are different than when I was growing up, I still believe the information I provide to each of them will help them know that the consequences to their actions can be more than they expected.

Being and having a mentor is a way to learn from each other and develop open communication.

In mentoring, we have to be role models, an example. Our behavior and lifestyle should be exemplary. We must possess the qualities that have affected them in a way that makes them want to be better people.

During the time with the young ladies we have done vision boards, along with celebrated birthdays and their accomplishments. We have attended a variety of events and experienced joining with other mentoring groups. We introduce them to things they may have never experienced, such as attending the Black Academy of Arts for different shows. I look forward to longevity with the young ladies even after they mature out of the program. I pray that they will each come back and be a mentor to the younger generation.

————————••●◉●••————————

# KNOW WHO YOU ARE

**Romans 8:16**, The Spirit himself bears witness with our spirit that we are children of God.

I did not know who I was or what I was supposed to do with my life. I had been made to feel less than, but I do not blame it all on others. I made myself feel less than. I definitely did not know my worth. I did not feel worthy of any good things. For a long time when good things would happen to me, I struggled with being happy about it because I did not feel that I deserved it.

When you know who you are, you know what you expect. You will not accept anything thrown at you. You know your worth and that you are valuable. I had to learn to control my temper when I felt disrespected.

I expected others to know what was unacceptable, but I did not show it. I did not know me enough to know to protect myself.

I did not recognize my value, which is a guide in our lives. I did not know my strength until I had to be strong. That was a lesson learned during the pain. After being in the shadow of someone for several years, it took years for me to get back to knowing my preferences, what motivated me, and the things that make up my character. It is more than how we think others see us, but more about how we think of ourselves. When we know ourselves, we are more confident and our self-esteem increases.

There is a benefit to knowing who you are. The greater the knowledge comes more choices. Self-awareness allows us to make better decisions that line up with our true selves.

Instead of being who others believe we should be, we honor our authentic self and chose what we know and trust is best for us.

Discover your own style, be your own brand.

Strive for self-knowledge which is an understanding of your feelings, motivations and thinking patterns. All of these have been a blessing to me in my continual growth.

———————————••●●●●••———————————

# APOLOGIZE TO YOURSELF

I forgive myself for allowing myself to be treated less than, for allowing myself to feel like I was less than because of my skin tone, my height or weight. I forgive myself.

I forgive myself for not speaking up for myself when I had plenty to say. For not being who I wanted to be even after knowing who that was. Although I did not know how, I refused to ask for assistance. In my younger years that would have meant I was weak. I did not have the knowledge. I would have been proving that those I thought felt that way about me, to be right. I forgive myself.

I forgive myself for not being the example I was created to be. I forgive myself for not being forgiving.

I would hold onto things that hurt me when I should have been talking to the person about it, so again it increased my anger. I now forgive myself.

I forgive myself for making a choice to be mean, and not dealing with my many issues.

In order to do so I had to have compassion, and understanding of why I needed to do so. I had to be willing to admit all that needed to be forgiven, all the wrongs, the mistakes, mishaps and misunderstandings. I had to make peace in order to move forward. I had to speak them out loud and say what I learned from it all. I forgive myself and I gave it a voice.

Journaling has helped me keep it all together, I have had to write out what had me so angry, and what I was willing to do about it.

It was up to me to execute the plan, but understand that God may change the plan, and many of times, He did. However, it was always in the best interest of myself.

I had to learn to be less critical of myself, and speak positive things into my life and surround myself with a positive environment. When the negative thoughts get in the way, I start to pray. Prayer changes things. I have had to be clear about some things and determine the best course of action.

I had to learn to do it afraid. Obey God in the face of fear. Having the courage to take action despite my fear. - Joyce Meyer

––––––––––••●●●●••––––––––––

# AFFIRMATIONS

**Romans 8:31,** If God is for us, who can be against us?

We are more than conquerors through Him who loves us.

I learned to speak words of affirmations to myself when I start mentoring. I thought I was doing it for the young ladies, but I was also doing it for myself. It blesses me to encourage myself as well as others. Speak over yourself positive words of encouragement daily. I would like to take this time and offer a few affirmations to you.

Tell yourself that you are,

'Fearfully and Wonderfully' made by God. Psalm 139:14

You are 'Loved and have a Purpose.' Psalm 57:2 God has a purpose for your life, He has numbered your days. And will fulfill every purpose He has for you.

You are in charge of how you feel and you choose happiness. Psalm 37:4 Take delight in the Lord, and He will give you the desires of your heart.

You do not have a need to compare yourself to others. You are 'Uniquely-You.'

Ephesians 2:10, For we are His workmanship, created in Christ Jesus for good works, which God prepared beforehand, that we should walk in them.

You can do all things through Christ that strengthens you. Philippians 4:13

You are more than enough and God provides you with more than enough.

2nd Corinthians 9:8, And God is able to make all grace abound toward you; that ye, always having all sufficiency in all things, may abound to every good work.

You are a change agent with the power to create change.

Joshua 1:9, have I not commanded you?

Be strong and courageous. Do not be frightened, and do not be dismayed, for The Lord your God is with you where you go.

Be the change you want to see.

Repeat, "I refuse to give up."

Galatians 6:9, let us not become weary in well doing, for at the proper time we will reap a harvest if we do not give up.

Jeremiah 29:11, for I know the plans I have for you, declares The Lord, plans to prosper you and not to harm you, plans to give you hope and a future.

2nd Timothy 1:7, For God hath not given us the spirit of fear, but of power, and of love, and of a sound mind.

# 23RD PSALM

V1, The Lord is Ella's Shepherd (Relationship)

She shall not want (Supply)

V2, He makes Ella to lie down in green pastures (Rest) He leads Ella beside the still waters (Refreshed)

V3, He restores Ella's soul (Healing)

He leads Ella in the path of righteousness for His name sake (Guidance)

V4, Yea though Ella walk through the valley of the shadow of death (Test)

She will fear no evil, for you are with her (Protection)

V5, You prepare a table before her in the presence of her enemies (Help)

You anoint Ella's head with oil (Consecration)

Her cup runs over (Abundance)

V6, surely goodness and mercy shall follow Ella all the days of her life (Blessed) and she will dwell in the house of The Lord forever. (Security).

---

# ABOUT THE AUTHOR

*Ella Jones* is the wife of Minister Marcus. L Jones Sr.

A bonus mom and grandmother. The home health care provider for her elderly mother and a servant for The Lord, living in expectancy. She enjoys being a mentor, having an effect on others by her lifestyle, supporting others in any way she can, and offering motivation to go higher. She has obtained her Associates degree in Criminal Justice, and often takes certification classes to better herself.

Ella is the Author of the 31 DAY DEVOTIONAL that offers Growth, Encouragement, and Inspiration. This was her first book, published March 2020.

She is the Founder and Director of PRECIOUS PEARLS (Women On The Move), an outreach ministry that provides food and clothing to those less fortunate. The group also visits those in nursing homes, playing bingo and dominos while offering prayer and spending time with them. Est in 2015.

Ella is also the Founder and Director of RUTH and NAOMI Youth Mentoring Program. The program is designed to work with young girls, ages 12-18 as they grow and develop into young ladies. Our purpose is to empower, motivate and inspire them to be the best version of themselves. Est in 2017.

Ella is elated to be a co-partner in ministry with her husband, Minister Marcus L. Jones Sr. "Yielded Vessels Ministries".

Est in 2016. We are Servants for the Kingdom of God.

# *Dale and Darlene*

# *Rest In Paradise*

# My Big Mama and I

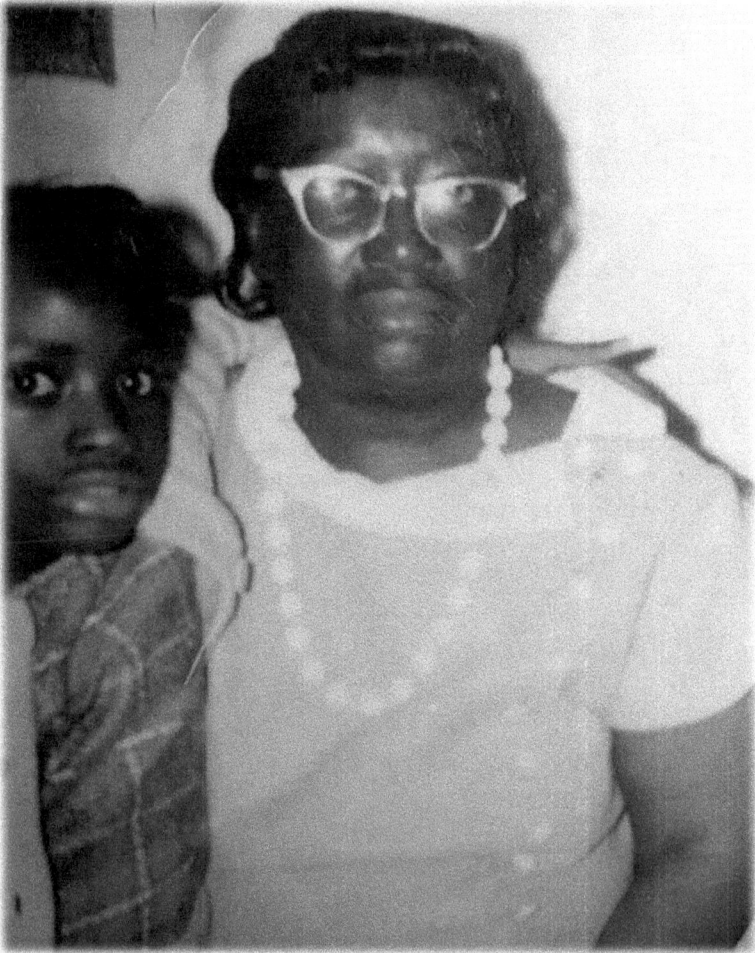

# *My Mother, Brother and I*

# *Marcus and Ella Jones*

# *Holding Strong*

# *Dec 30th 2007 to Present*

The title of the book came from a spiritual encounter in 2015.

It was my first time in Shreveport, Louisiana since leaving there after being born. I was in town for a conference with Minister Cynthia Diggs, and I was awakened at 5:17AM. The words I heard were, "If you release it I will release you."

That was the first time I would give my full testimony regarding my birth."

www.ingramcontent.com/pod-product-compliance
Lightning Source LLC
Chambersburg PA
CBHW070057100426
42740CB00013B/2866